AFTER THE STOP

HOW TO SURVIVE AFTER BEING STOPPED BY THE POLICE AND OTHER LESSONS TO MASTER THE GAME

E. Niketa Parker

Publisher

ABOUT THE AUTHOR

E. Niketa Parker is a Veteran, Former Law Enforcement Officer and Pastor of the Living Waters Ministries where he serves as Superintendent of the Southeast Birmingham Alabama District. He is a member of one of the largest Pentecostal denominations in the world, The Church of God in Christ, Intl. He is married, the Father of 1 child, 4 grandchildren and a tutor in the Birmingham City School System. He received his B.S. Degree in Criminal Justice at Troy University.

ACKNOWLEDGMENTS

I am very fortunate to be surrounded by supportive family members and friends. Without them, the writing of this book would not be possible. I am so appreciative for their love, longsuffering, laughter and understanding.

First to my immediate family: my mother, Mary Helen Parker; my father, Charles Arthur Parker; my two siblings: Yolondra (Lonnie) Austin, and Albrino Bell Parker. Special thanks to Stephanie Miller who was my first editor and accepted the assignment with glee.

To Latoya, my beautiful, precious, brilliantly talented daughter. My only child, my heart. I thank God for the young lady you have become every day.

Finally, I thank God for my gorgeous wife, Monica. We have been together since we were young adults. We grew together, loved together, cried together. Thank you for your overwhelming support in accomplishing this book.

Thank you for not giving up on me, being patient with me, believing in me, loving me! I love you all!

Thank you!!!

TABLE OF CONTENTS.

GETTING STARTED.

CHAPTER 1

INTRODUCTION

It's NBA All-Star weekend in Orlando Florida, The West vs. the East in the mid-season showdown. In Sanford Florida it's raining as a young 17-year-old walks to the nearest 7-Eleven for a snack. He purchases an Arizona ice tea and a pack of skittles and heads back home. As he enters the residential area, he notices a person following him. He walks faster as he talks to his girlfriend and tells her what is going on. A few minutes later, someone is heard screaming "help" 14 times, when gunshots ring out. The young man who simply wanted a snack lay dead. That young man was Trayvon Martin. His death would change everything.

On July 13, 2013, a travesty of justice happened in America. The Trayvon Martin case had come to an end of jury deliberations. The verdict is in, not guilty. For many in America this returned verdict was fair, others were disappointed tremendously, but for black America, it was business as usual. Many black Americans thought it was a victory that charges were brought up at all, but knew better than to hold their breath for a guilty plea.

Since that date, many lives have been lost. Names such as: Dontre Hamilton, Eric Garner, John Crawford, Michael Brown, Tanisha Anderson, Tamir Rice, Walter Scott and Freddie Gray.

At least one of these above-mentioned deaths played out for the whole wide world to see. A televised death of a man outside a store accused of selling loose cigarettes. We saw him as he screamed to the police that he could not breathe. We saw him begging for his life as the police ignored his fainting cries. We saw him take his last breath. What was his crime? Selling loose cigarettes. What was his sentence? Death!

Tamir Rice was in the park across the street from his house. He was playing with a toy gun. He was doing what little 12-year-old boys do, play with toy guns. The police were called and 3 seconds later little Tamir was dead. What was his crime? Playing in the park with a toy gun.

My purpose for writing this book is to help our children, brothers and sisters make it home safely, too survive. Plain and simple. It is my attempt to provide a framework for the targeted people of America, to have successful outcomes when encountering our law enforcement officers. This work isn't meant to be a literary masterpiece, but an easy to read guide for students and parents. Some students are very fortunate to have a parent to speak into their lives. To give positive and constructive instructions and help navigate them through life. Others have extended family or even friends to fulfill this role. This book is for those who have no one!

~Where do we go from here? Survival!~

This book, **How to Survive after Being Stopped by the Police and other lessons to Master the Game,** is a blueprint, a day-to-day guide for helping our youth survive on the mean streets of America. I feel many of our young people need to understand that there is a way to navigate the streets of America, interact with the police, maintain your individual dignity and return home safely.

In **How to Survive after Being Stopped by the Police and other lessons to Master the Game**, we will cover topics such as "Getting your head straight".

In this chapter we will ask the reader a simple question, who are you? We cannot move forward until we know the answer to this question. We are faced with generations of our youth growing up without knowing who they are. They are the innocent victims of fatherlessness, single parent homes, broken homes, the foster care system, homelessness, runaways, alcohol and drug addiction. Many of our youth who have either lived or been a part of these systems or culture are at a clear disadvantage of not knowing who they are.

The section entitled "<u>You are not what they say you are</u>" will address outside voices trying to define who you really are. Even though your appearance (dress, hairstyles and your ride) may be different from mainstream America, it doesn't make your differences wrong.

<u>How to Survive</u>: <u>Talking with "5-O"</u> is where we will give your son, daughter, grandson, granddaughter, nephew and niece the strategies needed to handle themselves when approached or confronted by concerned citizens or "neighborhood" watch and law enforcement officials. It is my belief that teaching your child to remain cool, calm and collected during the beginning of the conversation can save their life.

If you don't read or remember another sentence of this book, please embed this phrase in your mind, "be respectful". Respect will carry you where pedigree can't. Countless numbers of people have gotten out of tickets and difficult circumstances simply because they were respectful.

For instance, if you are pulled over by the police and your driver license is suspended, the police can legally take you to jail with no questions asked. Instead of blowing up, cursing and acting a fool, smile and keep calm. Remember the officer does not know you or your situation. Keep your hands in clear sight, answer his questions (the ones that pertain to your situation), listen carefully and be respectful.

As a young man, I have been pulled over my fair share of times. Most of the time the officer had me nailed, I was totally wrong and guilty. Nevertheless, I remembered to practice what my parents taught, "be nice and respectful, it can carry you a long way". As a result, I was let off with a warning.

This book is my attempt to help our generation of young African American youth and people of color, survive the terrible violence they encounter on a daily basis. It is my belief that every child that leaves home to gather with his friends or go to the corner store should return home safely.

Before we learn how to engage and interact with the police, I would like to take this opportunity to speak with you about how to Survive in the Game of Life.

The chapters that lie ahead are packed with information that can help you succeed in life. Study them, learn them, embrace them and pass them on.

GETTING YOUR HEAD STRAIGHT.

CHAPTER 2

WHO ARE YOU?

~*You are who God say's you are*~

Despite the challenges that you face on a daily basis, the hardships that you live with, the absence of a parent or loved one, you are not who they say you are. You might have grown up in the projects or ghettos of the city. You might not have enough food to eat at night. You might not have the latest fashions to wear to school. You might not get the best grades in school. You might not be able to talk as fast as everyone else. You might not even have a friend. People may put you down and even make fun of you. It's possible that you might fall into one or more of these categories, but one thing is sure, you are not who they say you are, but you are who God say's you are!

In the First - book of the Bible, Genesis, God created the heavens and the earth. He created the world and made the sun and the moon to shine on the earth. He made the lakes, rivers, mountains, valleys, plants and animals. Then, in Genesis 1:26 God created man and made him in His own image, after His likeness: and gave him dominion over the fish of the sea, the birds of the air and the animals on the land. After God created man and woman He blessed him and said unto them, be fruitful and multiply, replenish the earth and subdue it.

God has not made you to be a follower, or a slave, or to fit in with other people. God has made you to be a ruler, a leader, a thinker, a problem solver. He has empowered you with wisdom, knowledge, understanding, compassion and to have dominion over the earth. God says in His Holy Word that you are the "head and not the tail, above and not beneath", as a matter of fact, God says that you are a winner.

Don't waste your time following people who are not going anywhere in life. Don't listen to people who are not concerned about your success. Don't believe what the media says about you. The complexion of your skin or the area you live in does not determine or dictate your future. Whether you live in the Penthouse or the Projects, you are what God says you are. You can become whatever you desire in your heart if you only believe in yourself. Use your time wisely and conquer whatever is placed before you. As a matter of fact, God has made you to be more than a conqueror through Christ Jesus our Lord (Ro. 8:37). This means with the help and guidance of God nothing in this world can stop you from accomplishing the goals that God has planned for you. You can do it, just don't give up!

In Jeremiah 29:11 God says, "For I know the thoughts *and* plans that I have for you, says the Lord, thoughts *and* plans for welfare *and* peace and not for evil, to give you hope in your final outcome". Did you know that you are so important that God knows every hair that is on your head? Isn't it amazing to know that God, who sits high and looks low, has a plan just for you?

God has a plan of peace, love, joy and wholeness for your life. He wants you to prosper and be in good health, even as your soul prospers in Him. Here is the good news. While people are talking negative and planning your destruction, God is thinking about your future and planning a successful end.

~*You Are Destined For Greatness*~

You might be wondering, how can I be destined for greatness, I am just a young person. You might tell yourself that there is nothing great about me. Some people don't even acknowledge that I'm alive. Many don't believe I will achieve anything, while others view me as annoying. As a matter of fact, I don't even see myself as being capable of doing anything great. If you happen to feel this way, you are not alone. Many people feel that greatness is for someone else and AVERAGE is all they are capable of. Don't ever let people incarcerate you with how they perceive you to be. You must tell yourself "I am not who you say I am and I will not be enslaved by your point of view".

God has called you to greatness! If God said it, I believe it and that settles it! I choose to believe God. Self-doubt and criticism from others is part of the process. Many times during the course of life thoughts of inadequacy or self-doubt will rise.

In the first chapter of the book of Jeremiah God calls him into the ministry and he makes a profound statement. He tells Jeremiah "Before I formed you in the womb I knew [and] approved of you [as my chosen instrument], and before you were born I separated *and* set you apart, consecrating you; [and] I appointed you as a prophet to the nations".

Jeremiah responded that "behold, I cannot speak because I am a youth". Jeremiah thought that because he was young, inexperienced and fearful, God could not use him to spread His word and complete His will. Jeremiah was experiencing the same feelings you might have experienced, **self-doubt**. Why did God say this? Because He knew everything about Jeremiah and He knew Jeremiah would doubt himself and say he was too young to speak for God. But, what God was trying to tell Jeremiah was that I know you have greatness inside of you and no task given or criticism by other people will stop you. God knew you before you were born. He knows everything you are going through right now. He knows you might be struggling with school, making friends, being too tall, being too short, dealing with low self-esteem, feelings of inadequacy, drug or alcohol addiction, parental neglect or a single parent home. Whatever your situation is God knew that you would be faced with it. No matter how hard the situation you face looks, God has already made a way of escape for you. You will make it because **you are destined for greatness.**

GETTING YOUR HEAD IN THE GAME.

Having your head in the game is paramount to survival. Your skull is the crater or holding pen for your brain. Your brain is the central computer for the body. The purpose of the brain is to exert central control over the organs of the body. The brain receives information from other organs and then processes the information and responds accordingly. For example, your eyes see something that appears to be hot. Your arm reaches toward the object and the hand with fingers touches the object. If it is hot, a signal is immediately transferred to the brain and the brain sends another signal to the hand to let the object go.

What you put in your head determines your very survival. What you see determines where you go in life. What you see determines the path you take in life. What you see determines if you will take risks. What you think and how you perceive your surroundings is very important to your survival. In this section, I'm not referring to how others see you, but rather how you see yourself. Ask yourself these following questions: How do you see yourself right now? Where do you see yourself in 5, 10, 15, 20 years from now? What neighborhood do you see yourself living in? Do you see yourself married, with children? How will you support your family? Will you be self-employed or work for someone else? Will you invest in metals, stocks or bonds? Do you see yourself as a leader? Will you write a book? What if your plan fails, do you have a backup plan or a plan B?

All of the above questions are very important and having an education will help you answer them all.

CHAPTER 3
GET AN EDUCATION

Education is the process of facilitating learning, Knowledge, skills, values, beliefs, and habits of a group of people and are transferred to other people, through storytelling, discussion, teaching, training, or research. Education frequently takes place under the guidance of educators, but learners may also educate themselves in a process called autodidactic learning. (Wikipedia)

Getting knowledge in your head makes you ahead of the game; it puts you in the game of life. Going to school is not for chumps, or suckers, but rather it is for those who want to be ahead of the game. It is for the person who is looking to answer the questions of life. Your education or thorough learning of a particular subject matter will propel you into a life that you can only imagine. If you are in high school or college, stay there and get your diploma. Complete the task that is before you. Do not let anyone distract you or turn you around. Just because completing school is not important to others doesn't mean, you have to adopt their story. Stay the course. For example, if I want to go from Florida to California, I have to determine what date I want to travel, when I want to return and by what mode of transportation I will choose. Now, if my time is limited I must choose a method of transportation that will fall within those parameters. For example: If I have one (1) week of vacation coming to me, and I want to spend at least 5 days in California, the only option I have to travel is going to be by airplane. Why? There are buses that go to California as well as trains and cars. That's correct!

The distance from northwest Florida to southern California is 2112 miles. If I travelled at a rate of 70 miles per hour (mph), it would take me 30 hours to get there. That's without stopping for gas, food or even sleeping. Looking at the original conditions I imposed on myself, flying is the only way to go. Driving would not allow me to spend the whole 5 days in California. Yes, if I drove, I would certainly arrive in California, but it would take me much longer to get there and my stay would be cut short. If you know, where you want to go, education can be the vehicle to get you there faster.

The vehicle of education makes a lot of stops on the road to success. The further you ride on the education train the better chance of success you will have. It is important to remember that getting a degree is different from receiving an education. There are literally millions of people who go to college, sit in classrooms, and come out no smarter than when they started. They failed to grasp the idea of learning, the transferring of ideas, knowledge, skills etc. between people.

These people were only there to check a block and hope that a job will be available when they graduate. Whenever I'm talking about the value of education, I like to draw a diagram of 5 circles. There are 5 circles starting from the smallest to the largest. The smallest circle represents a GED or high school diploma. In this area, your earning potential is minimal which makes it very hard to support yourself, let alone a family. Minimum wage jobs fall into this category. The next largest circle represents an associate's degree. It is here where jobs, especially technical jobs, open up and pays significantly more. The third circle represents a bachelor's degree. This is the entry-level degree for most professional jobs. Salaries vary considerably, but this opens the door to supervisory and management jobs.

The fourth circle represents those with the coveted master or terminal degrees. It is called that because most people stop here on the educational train. If you chose the right field and posses the right master's degree, your salary will jump greatly. The final circle is the highest degree awarded which is the PhD. These salaries can be very lucrative and rewarding. The point being, the farther you go on the education train the more money and opportunities are afforded to you at each stop.

Now that we have chosen which field of study we want to pursue and boarded the right train, obtained our degree, now what's next? Many people have completed their education only to hear those dreaded six words "you do not have enough experience". I was faced with this obstacle when I completed my B.S. degree in Criminal Justice. Instead of getting mad and saying this school thing doesn't work, I decided to volunteer at the local Probation & Parole Office for free. Yes, I said for free. If you did not know, that is what volunteer means (for free!) Lol. After doing this for several months a job came open and I had the experience needed and the job was mine. I learned a long time ago that experience was experience. Whether it was paid or not, it still counted in the world of work as valuable experience. Therefore, as you pursue your goals don't be afraid to volunteer. It helps you to understand the type of work you will be doing and determine if it's the right fit for you.

CHAPTER 4

DREAM BIG

Before we go to the next chapter, I would like to share with you about **dreaming big.** I believe one of the biggest weakness in our American culture is that we have lost the ability to dream big. When I was a kid, we were taught to dream big, shoot for the moon! Our parents instilled in us the desire to be whatever your imagination could conjure up. We had kids that wanted to be astronauts, basketball players and fire fighters, all at the same time. The power of what could be propelled us to keep going.

One of the most heartbreaking things I ever heard was from one of my best friends Amos Taylor. Amos and I attended church together as well as hanging out at garage sales on Saturday mornings. Amos started teaching Sunday school at one of our public housing units for children whose parents had no transportation or worked and were unable to attend church. Amos asked the children what they wanted to be when they grew up, and one of the boys said all he wanted to be was a bus driver. When he told me that, it just broke my heart. Out of all of the things in the world to become, he could only dream of being a bus driver. Another young boy who lived in my neighborhood stated that when he grew up he wanted to be a garbage man. Now I'm not knocking those professions because my mother, Mary Helen Parker, told me all work is honorable. But parents please encourage your children to dream and dream big. Nothing is impossible to him that believeth. This is why education is so important. It unlocks limitations that are many times self-imposed and unleashes a world of possibilities.

CHAPTER 5
MAKING IT HAPPEN

Goal setting and follow through are two of the most important skills a person can develop in this lifetime. I can accomplish more things when I set goals. I often tell this story of what helped me get through college. I completed 1 year of college while in the military. After I returned home, I found a job and started college at nights. One of the first things I did was sit down with my academic advisor to discuss what and how many classes I needed to graduate. After she outlined what I needed, I took out a legal sheet of paper and wrote out every class I would need to take in order to graduate in 3 years. I then made copies and placed them in several places I would see every day. Whenever a class was completed, I scratched it out. This helped me to keep going and to stay focused. It also provided a roadmap for me to follow, and it worked.

Allow me to say this before I move on. A lot of people have great ideas and or goals in their head. They walk around with all these great ideas but never commit them to paper. In order to be successful in any area of your life you must have written goals. When goals are written down they become a blueprint that will lead you to your destiny.

Once your goals have been determined, follow them and don't give up. The road to success or fulfilling your dream gets long and lonely sometimes, but the key is to just follow through and don't give in.

GETTING PAID.

CHAPTER 6

PREPARING YOUR RESUME

For most of you, the term resume preparation is nothing new. I volunteer at a local middle school and assist kids arriving at school, mentoring male students and helping out in the Technology lab. Sixth and seventh graders are introduced to this and are actually creating their own resume while still in grade school. But for some of you who have not heard the term or aren't familiar with it, a resume is a document that you present to a future employer that describes your education, work history and accomplishments. It contains the date you began and ended working, the title or position of your job, duties performed, major accomplishments and awards received.

A resume is your opportunity to introduce yourself to a perspective employer (person who will hire you) and let him see what skills you have before an interview is scheduled. It is your time to shine on paper. A young lady who was applying for a summer position with the City of Birmingham and needed assistance completing the paperwork recently approached me. One of the items needed was a, you guessed it, resume. I started asking her basic questions about her background, school activities, community service, and grades. The only information she could put on her resume was that she attended school. All of the other areas mentioned above were completely blank. She had no information to share. Now that doesn't make her a bad person and given the chance, she might do a great job, but on paper or her resume, she would not be selected for an interview.

In order to survive on the mean streets of America you must be prepared. You must put the work in and document that work (resume) and the successes you had on the job or school. To have a resume you must have something to report about. If you are a student, get involved in your school. Find something at your school that interests you and join it. Whether it is sports or some school club, join in, you will love it. Also, get the best grades you possibly can. As a goal, strive to be on the A-B honor roll. This will make your parents and teachers very happy, and look nice on your resume. If you are looking for a job get involved in your community by joining a local church or boys and girls club organization. This shows that you are not only concerned about yourself but the welfare of other people and groups and looks great on your resume.

~Online Search Engines~

Now that you are getting good grades, participating in school based programs and working in your community, it's time to put that information into a resume. If you don't have a parent or teacher to help get you started, the internet will assist you greatly.

To search the website you have to use a search engine such as Google, Yahoo or Bing to name a few. Enter into the search box whatever topic you choose and the information comes up. Whether you are looking for "how to prepare a resume" or the "44th president", the internet can help you fulfill your goals.

Online search engines are also very useful in looking for jobs. Numerous job search sites can help you find people who are looking to hire you. In addition, the internet can be used to help research projects for school, college and work.

~Networking~

Webster defines networking as "the exchange of information or services among individuals, groups or institutions". The most effective way to find a job is by using this strategy of networking. Networking is nothing more than meeting people, finding things in common to talk about, staying in touch with that individual and hopefully being able to assist each other to achieve common goals in the future. Oftentimes the person that you are networking with knows someone else who can help you find the job that fits.

There are a great number of places to network and make contacts such as school board meetings, city council meetings, church, etc.

~Internships/Volunteering~

When you start looking for a job, many times the employer wants you to have some type of experience. This can be very tricky and frustrating at the same time. Here is the dilemma: in order to get experience I need a job, but to get a job I need experience. At this point, most people get frustrated and accept a position that they are over qualified for, doesn't pay enough, or just stop looking altogether. But fortunately for you I have a strategy that you can use to overcome this, it's called using "internships or volunteering".

Volunteering means working for someone for free. You might ask why in the world would anyone want to do that? I'm glad you asked. First of all, volunteering allows you to test the waters to see if you even want to work at that particular job or in that field of work. Secondly, volunteer experience is also counted exactly like paid experience. You get to learn the job and your pay is the experience you get to list on your resume. Internships are usually worked while in school and could or could not be paid, but still provide the experience you need to list on your resume.

~Social Media~

You are almost ready for that interview, but before you go let's talk social media. Social media is very popular these days. It seems everyone wants to tell the world how they feel, share how they spend their time, and show how they dress. On the surface this seems great but that little bit of fun can come back to haunt you down the road. Many companies are now using your social media profiles to see just what type of person wants to work for their company. If you have information that is offensive to other people "take it off". Jobs are not easy to find these days and losing the opportunity to work because you want to display information that some might feel is offensive is simply not worth it.

~Dress to Impress~

There is an old saying "first impressions are lasting impressions". When you leave out of your house people are going to judge you on your appearance. The way you dress gives people a glimpse into your mind and the way you see yourself. Take the time to groom yourself properly especially when going to a job interview. The employer is looking for someone who is not only qualified to do the job, but also represents his company.

Remember, you are the one looking for a job not the company. Dressing for a job interview is not the same as going out with friends or hanging out at home. Please listen carefully. Do not bring your personal style and taste to the interview environment. Trust me, it will not be appreciated or understood. Put yourself in the shoes as an employer. If you owned a Hip-Hop clothing store and hired a person to work in the store, you would expect them to show up on time, do some work when they get there and look sharp. If the person you hired showed up with full metal clothing, Goth clothing, or clothing with satanic symbols you would consider that inappropriate and wrong. **Right**? **Why**? Because it's a Hip-Hop clothing store. You would expect them to reflect the image of the store.

Make sure your hair is groomed, clothing clean and ironed. For the guys, please pull your pants up to your waist, wear a belt, and have clean shoes. For the gals, please make sure your blouse or dress is not too low, too tight, or too short below. Remember you're dressing for a job interview not to meet people at a club. If you follow these quick little rules you should be ready to make a nice first impression and compete with anyone for the job.

~*Follow Up*~

One of the most important steps after the interview is following up. This step is often overlooked because of ignorance of the game. Many people think that their presentation was so great that the interviewer would never forget them, nevertheless, you can never take things for granted when looking for a job. The follow up or thank you letter is another opportunity to showcase your talents. It is one last opportunity to get in front of the decision maker and let them see why you are the best person for the job. This letter should be short and to the point. First, start with a line or two thanking them for the opportunity to see you. Next, remind them of why you are the best person for the job with three to five short sentences, and finally leave your contact information again for any further questions they may have. That's it! Sending a thank you letter could ultimately be the tiebreaker between you and your closest competition. By taking the extra initiative (step) you are showing your future boss that you have what it takes to succeed in their organization. In addition, if you are having trouble writing a thank you letter, just Google it. There are thousands of templates and examples to follow for free.

TALKING WITH "5-O".

The motto of the police force is to "protect and serve"

CHAPTER 7

1ST CONTACT

~Be respectful~

Being pulled over is a very stressful moment for most people. As we see in the media today, some police officers are being extremely disrespectful and intolerant of certain communities during routine police stops. Some of these stops are resulting in people being belittled, harassed, intimidated, disrespected, beaten and arrested and some even resulting in death. This is why you must remain calm and respectful. You have no way of knowing what the officer has encountered before stopping you, nor should you have to, but being respectful can lower the anxiety level of most people. I know most of you are saying we have so many media examples of people not breaking the law and getting slammed, kicked and punched. My response to that is what is the alternative? What will happen if you start throwing blows with the police or trading insults? I can sum that up in one word, disaster. You cannot win using street tactics against the police. In fact, that is what some of them are counting on, so just remain respectful. Also no cursing and always use a respectful tone.

Many of our young people today simply don't think cursing or the use of profanity in public or around authority figures is wrong.

Some young people have never been taught that profanity is vulgar and they fail to see how using vulgar language makes people feel disrespected. If you fall into that category then I am here to inform you that it is wrong and can only cause your encounter with the police to go wrong.

~Ask why you are being pulled over~

You have a legal right to know why you are being engaged by the police. Asking why you were stopped serves notice to the police that you are not assuming (giving in to) guilt. You need them to tell you what the issue is first, and then you can address it. Many times the cops are pulling people over to try to find a reason to further investigate some form of wrongdoing (I have been told this by former cops). I mention this because in some communities DWB (driving while black) is reason enough to be considered breaking the law in some form or fashion. You must know, not assume, why they are pulling you over. Suppose they pulled you over because of a tail light being out or you were swerving and you started the conversation out by saying " I know I was speeding officer because…" Now instead of discussing the real reason he stopped you, you've given them a legitimate reason for the stop. **Always ask why**.

~Hands first~

Always keep your hands visible when stopped by cops. This makes them less nervous when approaching a vehicle. There are many horror stories about cops approaching a car and getting shot for no reason at all. So, rightfully, they are on guard at all times. Don't be silly, put yourself in their shoes. For this reason, I recommend that all parents place their "papers" (car registration and insurance documents) in an envelope above the visor. That way you or your child cannot be blamed for reaching into the glove box trying to pull a gun on the officer. Always ask the officer for permission before reaching for anything. Don't assume or take anything for granted. This is a very tense moment you are in and you want to be able to walk away unharmed. One of my good preacher friends stated that when he is pulled over the first thing he does is put both of his hands outside the window to show the officer he has nothing threatening in his hand. Remember the goal is to make it home safely.

When asked for I.D. , ask the officer what he wants you to do. Tell the officer you are getting whatever he is asking for before you reach for it. Hopefully, you have your documents above you and the officer will not be confused as to whether you are reaching for something suspicious. Remember, the officer doesn't know you and may have had a bad day or could just be biased toward people in general or could just be scared. This could be put your life in jeopardy and having a clear conscious conversation is necessary. You are required to present your license, registration and insurance documents upon request or demand.

With that being said, have your information ready and current. There is no reason for people to drive around with expired drivers, suspended or revoked license. Well to be honest, sometimes we just forget they expired, but I digress. Make sure you have a current vehicle registration in your car. Parents if you are lending your child the car for the day, please take the responsibility of ensuring that you have current car tags. The last thing you would want is for your child to be detained or getting a ticket because you did not make sure the business of driving a car was handled.

Lastly, please, please and please do not operate your vehicle without the proper insurance. If you drive without insurance and get stopped, it is an automatic fine. This fine can range from $100.00 to $500.00 for the first offense. Many states are also reporting you to the dept. of motor vehicles, and they will suspend your registration and add a fine up to $200.00 per vehicle that is uninsured. If your documents are in order it can make this traffic stop a lot faster and smoother.

~Make sure you put the officer at ease~

Now that you have all your papers in order and they are above your head, the next step is to put the officer at ease. Remember he is already tense. A smile goes a long way. Ask the officer how his day is going. This move is very, very important because when you are relaxed, it tends to relax those around you. Think of this moment as your audition for a big part in a movie or commercial. You will be playing the part of the driver who is minding his or her own business and headed to your local grocery store. All of a sudden, you see blue lights behind you. At first, you think the cop is going to pass on, but he is still on your bumper and you finally pull over. As the officer is getting out of his car, you start to replay the last few minutes in your mind wondering if you broke any laws. As he approaches the vehicle he has his hand near his gun and ask you the magic question," do you know why I pulled you over?" Action! Now if you're like me, by now you're aggravated and wondering why he is pulling me over; I've got places to go, people to see and things to do. I know I haven't broken any rules, my tags are current and I have insurance. By now your inner feelings of anger start manifesting outwardly with frowns and side eyes. LOL. What are you going to do? I'll tell you what you're going to do, **SMILE.** That's right, give the officer the biggest smile you can give. Why? Because a smile automatically makes others around you feel warmer and makes you seem more trustworthy. (Huffington Post 2/8/15) Remember, he is already tense and a smile goes a long way.

~Never admit any guilt~

The officer will ask you do you know how fast you are going? Answer, how fast was I going officer? Or did you know you were going 45 in a 35? Answer; is that what your radar says? Remember, in admitting to going just 1 mile over the speed limit, you are legally guilty of breaking the law. If he ask you do you know why I pulled you over, answer no, because you really don't know why!

~Attitude~

If you want to tick off the police, just start out with attitude. I recently spoke to a police officer and he stated the worst thing you can do is give the officer attitude. Fewer tickets have never been written because the citizen had a bad attitude. What is attitude? It can be as little as a look or giving face to a cop. It can be refusing to let your window down and have a conversation with the cops. It could be refusing to put out your cigarette when asked by the police. Many times when people are pulled over, especially between 12am and 4am, the officers may assume they have left a club or party scene where drinking has been going on. Refusal to roll your window down and/or put a cigarette out is often construed (thought of) as trying to hide alcohol or drug usage. We have to remember that not all cops are on a witch-hunt and are simply trying to do their jobs. I myself, as well as many of you, have a vested interest in proper policing. If I or one of my loved ones is driving around town, we want the added security to know that drunk drivers and those under the influence of drugs are being taken off the streets and arrested before they cause a tragic accident.

~Don't get smart with the police, you cannot win~

Statements like I'm tired of you guys pulling me over, why are you picking on me, or stopping me. You just stopped me yesterday and you know I'm clean, are only going to add fuel to the fire. Don't let the officer know that he is getting under your skin. Even if he is getting on your last nerve and all those things are true, keep all those comments in your head. Your goal should be to end the police stop and go on about your business.

~Don't make faces, sounds, or comments~

Ladies don't roll your eyes or get sarcastic, or say "whatever". Guys please don't tell the officer he is tripping. Keep your cool, this is very serious business. This is not a TV show and things could get dangerous in a split second. If you don't keep your cool you could be facing a misdemeanor or felony, which if convicted, can seriously affect the rest of your life. A felony conviction means you are not allowed to vote, serve as jurors, restricts your ability to visit foreign countries, own a gun, work in certain career fields, curtail parental benefits, especially during custody battles and the ability to receive SSI, food stamps, state or federal grants, receive federal cash assistance and live in public housing. A felony is serious business.

~Listen carefully~

Only speak when spoken to. This is not the time to ramble on or fill in the blanks. Simply comply with the officers request (remember no searches at all).

~Everything you say is on the record~

The officer is recording the whole traffic stop, from beginning to the end. He has a microphone on his body to protect him from false accusations, but to also prove what actually happened on the traffic stop. These microphones are extremely sensitive. Be sure that you and/or your friends are not talking during this stop. You are facing something, which could turn into a very hostile and dangerous situation in a matter of seconds. One word or sentence taken the wrong way, or misheard can shift the mood of the officer and alter the outcome of a traffic stop or any engagement with cops.

This brings me to something my parents taught me years ago, **"be careful who you hang with"**. If you are cool, calm and collected, you have a tendency to hang around with people who are the opposite of you. I had a friend growing up who was loud, crazy, very outgoing, and said anything that came into his head and didn't care what anyone thought about him. He would often get into confrontations with complete strangers just for fun. If stopped by the police a person with that type of personality could cause a simple traffic stop to go wrong. Make sure you know the people in your car. If you know the person you are hanging with smokes weed, then you had better think twice before riding with or letting them ride with you. Everyone wants to project a gangster image around their friends. They often say they don't care what the police do and I'll serve time before I snitch or give someone up. Let me be the first to tell you that this is all just a bunch of **CRAP.** These people are usually the first ones to squeal like a pig when brought under a little pressure. My nephew was driving his car and riding 4 deep when he was pulled over by the police. He was clean but one of his boys was riding dirty (had drugs). One of the guys in the back seat threw the drugs near my nephews' driver seat so he wouldn't get caught. He was quickly put in check and decided to take the responsibility for his own actions. Let me be the first to say I'm grateful he took the rap, but this is not how the story usually ends. So be careful who you hang around, it could cost you your freedom.

~Police cars are equipped with dash cameras~
Police cars are equipped with dash cameras also that continue to roll until the traffic stop is over or turned off. All of your actions are also being recorded and can be used for court. Everything you do is being recorded. In North Carolina it is up to the authorities to decide if they want to show the video to the public.

~You can equip your car with a dash camera also~
Dash cameras are very inexpensive and can help protect you against false accusations. We will talk about this later.

~When you are questioned by, the officer be polite~
Answer yes or no. Not yea or what or huh or naw. This is no time to use street language or hood talk. Be sure to speak up because you want to be understood.

~Make sure you tell the truth, the whole truth and nothing but the truth~

The officer is listening and making notes of your conversation. Plus it is being recorded. When he/she leaves you and return, they will probably ask you some of the same questions previously asked to see what your response will be. If you tell the truth, you won't have to remember a lie. Lying to an officer is a criminal offense and if they choose to you could be arrested.

~Do not volunteer any information it will not help your case~

Police are great at putting the pieces of a puzzle together. Trying to give them partial info will only come back and haunt you later.

~Respect authority~

First of all respect means to regard someone highly; an attitude of admiration or esteem. It is very hard for people to respect anyone who they perceive as giving them a hard time or not letting them have their way. In the military, we respected the rank that was on someone's shoulder. It was something they earned (sometimes lol). It is our job as parents to teach our children to behave in a certain manner in public and to respect adults. In my opinion, this is the crux of our problems in America, a lack of respect. I volunteer at a local school about one day a week. I have witnessed firsthand just how disrespectful children can be, not only towards themselves but teachers and administrators also. If you want to know why our children aren't learning, here it is: a lack of respect for authority. So many of the children come into school with chips on their shoulders and bad, extremely bad attitudes. They walk down the hallways disorderly, cursing and refusing to adhere to instructions and this is at 7 a.m. in the morning. Once they enter the classroom, teachers spend the majority of their time trying to bring the class to order. The other children who are respectful and follow the rules sit in disgust because all of their time is being wasted due to their disrespectful classmates. If we are going to change our class-rooms and society, we must first start with teaching our children to respect authority. This must and can only begin in the home.

In the meantime, we must, as a neighborhood or society, teach that respecting authority doesn't mean you have to agree with what they are saying or doing. Some people abuse the authority given to them by their superiors. Police officers are given authority by the state they reside in and the jurisdiction they serve. As we know from the news lately, some officers' conduct has come into question; which have led to numerous deaths of citizens, particularly those of African American descent. I believe in order for us to reduce so many police stops from going bad we must teach our children to have respect for authority. This does not abdicate law enforcement or any in authority from being descent, honorable, fair or honest and neither does it excuse them from upholding the oath they take as officers, which is to "protect and serve".

Romans 13:1-3 says, "Everyone must submit to governing authorities. For all authority comes from God, and those in positions of authority have been placed there by God. Therefore, anyone who rebels against authority is rebelling against what God has instituted, and they will be punished. For the authorities do not strike fear in people who are doing right, but in those who are doing wrong. Would you like to live without fear of the authorities? Do what is right and they will honor you." (NLT)

At the end of the day you can only control the things you have control over. You must control your actions and hold those in authority accountable for theirs.

~We must teach our children not to be tricked into becoming angry and hostile~

Some officers already know that because of the history of racial discrimination, racial profiling and police brutality, there is an undercurrent of distrust and uneasiness. With this in mind, it is imperative that we teach our children not to disrespect officers in uniform. Sometimes, they may try to goad or tempt you into this area to open the door for further questions and detainment. Some officers use vulgar language and racial undertones to bait you into losing your cool. Remember to stay calm. It's not what someone calls you but what you answer too.

~Follow orders~

If the officer asks for your driver's license, by law you must give it to him. If he asks for your registration and insurance, you're obligated to present this info to him as well. Always do it with a smile. If he asks you to exit the vehicle, just comply. But if he asks to search you or the vehicle, that's where you draw the line. You have a constitutional right to not allow anyone to search your vehicle. If this is a simple traffic stop, you are not normally asked to exit your vehicle. If he states he must search you for "officer" safety, you must comply, but make it known to the officer that you disagree with what he is doing.

~Don't lose your cool~

If you are obeying the laws and not riding dirty or have a warrant for some other situation, then you have no reason to lose your cool. Pay attention to what is going on. Look for the officers' name and badge number. If you cannot make it out just remember to get the car number and remain cool. Any blatant act of questioning the officer can lead to a longer traffic stop. Be Cool.

CHAPTER 8

TO SEARCH OR NOT TO SEARCH.

Under the 4th amendment, we are protected by the constitution against unlawful search and seizure and makes arbitrary police car searches illegal. If your vehicle is searched without your permission or a valid reason, your rights have just been violated. Under the 4th amendment, courts generally give the police more leeway to search a vehicle rather than a home. Known as the automobile exception to the search warrant requirement, individuals have less of an expectation of privacy when driving a car.

*The police can search your car under the following circumstances:

a. You have given the officer consent.
b. The officer has probable cause to believe there is evidence of a crime in your vehicle.
c. The officers reasonably believe a search is necessary to their own protection (a hidden weapon, for example).
d. The officer has a valid search warrant.

www.traffic.findlaw.com

An officer can conduct a warrantless search in areas that are within your reach including the glove dept. and any area of the front seat, if the officer suspects weapons or a potential threat.

*Plain View Doctrine

Officers are also allowed to search if they see something in plain view.

The **plain view doctrine** allows an officer to seize without a warrant – evidence and contraband found in plain view during a lawful observation. This doctrine is also regularly used by TSA Federal Government Officers while screening persons and property at U.S. airports.

For the plain view doctrine to apply for discoveries, the three-prong *Horton* test requires:

1. The officer to be lawfully present at the place where the evidence can be plainly viewed.
2. The officer to have a lawful right of access to the object, and
3. The incriminating character of the object to be "immediately apparent."

~Giving consent~

Consent is giving someone permission, in this case, to search your car or person. Under no circumstance are you to give permission to search.

Don't get tricked by the reasons the officer is going to give you for searching your vehicle.

They will say things like: people are selling guns around here, do you mind if we search your car? There has been a lot of drug activity do you mind if we search your car? There was a robbery in the area do you mind if we search your car? Also remember when you refuse a search the officer will hit you with this: You must be hiding something, if not, let us search.

Now remember, if the officer demands to search your car, he will usually ask you to step out of the car and place you in the back of the police car.

Sometimes you will be placed in handcuffs (for officer safety) of course. If this happens to you do not get upset, but say to the officer that you do not consent as he is walking you to his vehicle. Remember, the cameras are rolling, and hopefully so is yours. More about that later.

What happens if you give an officer the permission to search your vehicle?

If you let them search, they will. Many young people mistake their encounter with the police with the ones they have at home. When your parents ask you if you did your homework and you say yes, most will not check it and take you at your word. The police are not the same way. Don't think because you consented they will go away, they won't. It's sad to say that you have some officers that are so narrow minded and hard up to look good and make arrests, that they will stop, detain and even plant evidence on innocent people.

Giving permission simply opens up the floodgates of consternation. You have a constitutional right to say no to a search. It's called the 4th amendment. Once permission is given for a search, there is no turning back. The officer has the right to turn your car upside down and inside out. There are too many instances to mention about how seats in cars have been removed, everything in the trunk thrown out and even seats torn with knives. The sad part is after the search is over and they find nothing, they usually just drive off, without an apology, and leave you to deal with the mess. If they suspect you have used drugs or are under the influence of drugs and cannot find anything, the dogs are called in to sniff things out. This unit is called the K-9 unit.

What are the dangers of consenting to a search?

Well let's start with the obvious one to me and that would be the police find something in the car that does not belong to you. As we all know, young people have been known to carry items that are not legal to carry. Let's look at two examples that support not consenting to a search of your vehicle. In our first example, let's say a young man is going out with some friends to see a movie and grab a pizza afterwards. He goes by and pick up friend (A) who rides shotgun. Next, they pick up friend (B &C) and head to the movies.

After the movie, the guys head to the local pizza shop. Friend (A) has moved to the back and swapped places with friend (C). On the way, the guys are stopped by local police for failing to use a signal. During the stop, the officer suspects something is going on and asks the driver if he would consent to a search of the vehicle. The driver, who has known his friends all of his life consents to a search. All the guys are asked to exit the vehicle and instructed to sit on the curb. During the search, the officer finds nothing in the front seat, but discovers a small joint in the rear of the car on the floorboard under the front seat near the back of the rear floor mats. The officer ask the boys whose joint is it, which no one claims ownership. The officer states if no one accepts responsibility they all will be arrested and go to jail. This story is all too familiar with young people. First and foremost, this writer does not support or endorse the use of drugs, period. All too often people are faced with this situation because they trusted their friends, didn't know they used drugs or thought they would get away with it.

For our last example, a young man borrows his brother's car and goes for a quick run to the local pizza parlor. He realizes he is going too fast when he sees the blue lights in his rearview mirror. The officer approaches the car and asks for his papers, which he hands the officer promptly. As the officer is handing the ticket to the driver, he asks him does he have anything in the car that he should know about? The young man answers "no" to the officer. He presses him a little more and tells him that if he tells him now that there is something in here, he will let him go with a warning. The young man refuses to give consent and the officer tells him he is free to leave. When the young man gets home, he tells his brother what happened and goes to eat his food. The brother immediately goes outside and opens his trunk to retrieve his coat. Inside the coat was a small bag of drugs.

To some, these stories might seem fictional, but I'm here to tell you that this type of thing happens daily. The previous two examples are perfectly good reasons why you do not give consent to a search of your vehicle. Two innocent lives could have been ruined by forfeiting your 4th amendment rights.

CHAPTER 9

AREN'T THE POLICE OUR FRIENDS?

Over the years the police have been portrayed as "officer friendly", always there to help little old ladies, kids who are lost and arresting the bad guys who committed some crime. These are good qualities that all law enforcement officers should have. Many officers are very friendly. They coach little league games, volunteer at homeless shelters, they feed the hungry, work in the big brother & sister programs, excellent fathers, mothers, sons, daughters, uncles and aunts. But the question still remains, are the police our friends? When it comes to traffic stops or any other type of engagements, the answer is a resounding No!

They are there to decide if you've done something wrong and whether they can arrest you to "enforce the law." When approached by the police listen carefully to the questions being asked. Usually, the officer asks with a smile on his face, "Do you know why I pulled you over?"

Whatever you do, don't answer this question with a yes, because it's a trap!

Maybe you *do* know. Maybe you don't, but might have a feeling that you were speeding or you swerved a little ways back. The average person would answer yes. Instead, answer with another completely honest answer: "No, sir/ma'am. I don't."

If you answer this question, it's already game over. You've admitted your guilt.

Anything you say will be used against you at court. The officers know how to craft a story from your own words. After the first few moments with you at the car, this is also a common time for the officer to start asking other "friendly" or seemingly harmless questions.

"Where are you coming from?"

"Where are you headed?"

"What are you up to tonight?"

These kinds of questions seem like friendly small talk to you, but they are actually probing questions. The officer is gathering any information she/he can to build a case against you. Riskology.co/traffic

The police are banking on you not knowing your rights and in order for them to increase the fine; they need you to incriminate yourself. I think the best way to answer these questions would be to just ask the officer "how can I help you officer?" Remember, don't be disrespectful, and stay cool. If he proceeds and starts saying why aren't you answering the questions, if you are a minor, remind the officer that you are a minor and that you need your parents present to answer any questions. Next ask the officer the million-dollar question, **Am I free to go?**

This questions cuts to the chase and forces the officer to either arrest you, give you the ticket or set you free. Remember; never leave until the officer says that you are **free to go.**

~Be aware of scare tactics~

If we find something, you are going away for a long time, if you tell me now I can help you.

~Beware, police can legally lie~

I'll talk to the D.A. and cut you a deal. The only person who can cut you a deal is the D.A; a beat cop doesn't have that type of authority.

~Staying calm~

This can be a very nerve racking time (tense).

~Comply with orders given~

(Such as sit here, stand here, stop walking) remember don't talk, **listen. This is not the time to try to show the officer or your friends that you are a man and will not be intimidated**. Your fight will never be won on the streets; it must be won in the courthouse.

~Ask if you are being detained again~

You want every camera or recorder to here you state that comment over and over again. You cannot be arrested for asking that question.

If not detained, ask, am I free to go?

~Here come the dogs~

If all else fails and the officer is determined to find something or is just ticked off because you are being intelligently defiant but compliant he will call for the K-9 unit. Just sit tight, remain calm and let what happens, happen. At this point, you cannot stop the officers from bringing the dog or the dog from alerting on your vehicle. Stay cool.

The police have stopped me a few times in my life as both a young man and an older one. At every engagement with the police, I have never had one instance of trouble. Yes I was ticketed a couple of times, and not shown any courtesy once, but I can't help to believe that because I stayed calm, cool and respectful made all of the difference.

RIDING CLEAN.

CHAPTER 10
INSPECT YOUR RIDE.

I t is a very good idea to inspect your car before it is taken for a ride. Many times, we are unaware of minor maintenance issues that need addressing. When I was in the military before we could drive a government vehicle, we had to inspect it first. This inspection involved at least 2 people and started from the front bumper to the rear. We had to check the oil, radiator, wiper fluid, brake fluid, belts, hoses, headlights, turn signals, brake and backup lights. Back then, it seemed like a waste of time, but now I see the wisdom of that rule.

Checking all of the above items ensured the longevity of the Governments vehicle, resulted in less major repairs, and cost savings to tax payers. I recommend before letting your teenager drive your car you do the following:

~Prepare yourself before you leave by inspecting your car/truck~
A few minutes of inspection can save you an hour of frustration and a costly ticket.

~Check your lights~
Make sure the brake lights, turn signals, backup lights, and headlights are all working.

~Check your papers~

Make sure you have an updated insurance coverage and car registration in an envelope and placed above the sun visor with a big clip. If the sun is out and the visor is pulled down, the paperwork will stay in place. Remember this is an important place to secure your documents so that if pulled over, you will not look suspicious when reaching for the requested papers.

~Check your gas~

Please make sure you have enough gas to go and return from your event. Running out of gas, especially at night, can be very dangerous and bring about unwanted attention.

~Check your friends~

If you suspect or know one of your friends has or uses illegal drugs or carries alcohol, and is a minor, you had better check them for your own safety.

~Get a dash camera~

As I stated earlier, police officers cars as well as themselves, are equipped with cameras. These cameras are supposed to help protect the officer and civilian from false accusations and provide a digital testimony of events that unfolded during an incident. Too often, the evidence from these cameras are hidden for a while, tampered with or even lost. I have a solution for that; buy your own dash camera. For as little as $100.00, you can buy your own dash-cam that will record everything said as well as seen during a traffic stop. These cameras can be set to record at various intervals and will record outside as well as inside your vehicle at the same time. Remember you have the responsibility of providing a vehicle that adheres to the laws of the road. It is not your child's area of responsibility to make sure the car has lights, bulbs and car insurance. Give any kid the keys to the car and the only thing he might ask you is if there is gas in it. Lol.

IN THE HOOD.

CHAPTER 11

CHOOSE YOUR FRIENDS WISELY.

P art of growing up as a kid is having friends and forming life-long friendships. Playing in the streets, hanging out at each other's houses and spending the night are still a part of growing up. Just as forming friendships and hanging out are still a part of our culture, it is just as important now, as it was then, to choose your friends wisely. Here are a couple of pointers to help you survive in the hood:

~Avoid confrontations: Personal, Social Media~
Having disagreements with friends is a part of life, but how you deal with those disagreements is crucial. If you are a parent you must decide how your want child will respond to bullying, threats or general shoving and pushing. I cannot impose my belief system in any way or fashion, but parents must decide how they want their child to respond. My response is to simply to stay away from confrontations. When they see a conversation going wrong, it's best to cut it off and remove themselves from that environment.

In addition, social media is a part of just about everyone's life these days. Words and images are displayed on peoples' news feeds and twitter accounts. People have become so passionate about their profiles and the online respect factor. In my time, you only had to worry about the neighborhood or school kids acting up, but today everyone is vulnerable to worldwide confrontations. No one wants to be injured because of a discussion that gets out of hand concerning a video, song or some puppy love interest. No one! Please beware of the dangers of words spoken or repeated on social media.

~*Learn how to walk away*~

There is power in walking away. It takes more guts to consider the consequences of your actions in advance and walking away than throwing caution to the wind.

~*Don't use drugs, or alcohol*~

If you are a student or young adult there are consequences of using drugs and alcohol or even hanging out with people who do. Using drugs is a decision that can lead to a broken, useless and wasteful life. Alcohol and drugs will hinder and kill your dreams. If you are a parent let your kids know that drugs will even stop them from dreaming. Be a broken record. This cannot be repeated enough.

~*Don't carry weapons*~

I know that we have the right to carry a gun but I don't think that it is a good idea. There are too many variables that can cause a simple traffic stop to go horrible. We as humans should practice to live peaceable with our neighbors.

~*Get in early*~

Lastly, remind your children, rather demand that your children get in the house early. Hanging out late at night only invites trouble. Instead of hanging out, they need to be investing in their own education. You don't have to have a lot of money as a parent to make sure your child gets an education. Use the internet or go to your public library. Use that time as family time to bond and grow closer.

As a young adult you often think that the party doesn't start until midnight. My wise father once said, " if you cannot get done what you want to get done by midnight, you don't have nothing to do". Lol It took me a number of years before I figured out what he meant. Hanging out late just invites a second look by the police. If you must be out, stay safe.

CONCLUSION.

Being pulled over or interacting with the police is an experience that most people have to deal with at some point in their life. It is the aftermath of those experiences that come to the forefront, which matters. What we are witnessing today is a lack of respect, decency and humanity towards each other.

There is a toxic environment in our nation today. People are divided along racial lines, it seems, more now than ever. This hatred does not start with the police dept., and must not be perpetuated by them, but at homes across this great country of ours. Parents must return to teaching respect for one another in their homes.

Where is the respect that my parents taught and instilled in me? Being black and raised in the Deep South used to be all about respect. My parents taught me to respect everyone, regardless of the color of their skin. We were not taught to say yes, maam or no sir to anyone. Yes or no would suffice as a sign of respect. We were taught that we weren't better than anyone else and no one was better than us.

My parents taught us to help those who were in need. To be kind, affectionate and preferring to help others before ourselves. We were taught to look for the good in everyone we came in contact with. Respect.

Police officers have a very tough job. Often it comes with low pay, long hours, short vacations, unappreciated by staff and the public, low morale, a high divorce rate, loneliness, depression ... it's a tough job. In policing you have to deal with people who are mentally disturbed, uneducated about the law, unconcerned, violent, and plan old law breakers; but with that being said, officers are still supposed to show respect and treat every individual as a human being. Officers are trained to de-escalate tense situations, not to inflame them. If the job is too stressful then they should just find work that is more suitable.

I never thought in a million years I would see the type of policing seen today in our media. In July 2016 an innocent man taking care of a client with autism, was confronted by the police because someone called and said a person had a gun. Police responded and confronted two men. The black man, who happened to be the caretaker of the person with autism, lay down in the street with both of his hands in the air. He explained the situation to the officers but was shot anyway. When he asked the officer "why did you shoot me", the officer responded, "I don't know". The victim did everything right in this situation and was still shot. Thank God, he was able to live and tell the story

In my opinion, this officer failed to see the good in what another person was doing. He failed to show kindness to a fellow human being. He failed to exercise common sense and abused the authority he has been entrusted with. This officer displayed a lack of respect for another human being.

What we are witnessing on a mass scale in this country is a lack of decency towards humanity. What is decency? Webster defines it as "behavior that conforms to accepted standards of morality or responsibility."

Police officers are trained in Standards and Ethics at the academy. Standards are minimum guidelines that you are to adhere to and ethics are moral principles that guide a person or group.

Law enforcement has standards that guide there interaction with the citizens of this great country. We as citizens expect not only a standard or uniform conduct from our law enforcement, but a moral compass to go along with it. We understand that if an officer pulls us over we must present identification upon request. We understand that we have a 5th amendment right not to incriminate ourselves and not be intimidated, coerced or forced by officers to answer certain questions. We even understand the toxic atmosphere we live in and the uneasiness of the police. We understand they have a dangerous job that must be done. What we don't understand is why certain people (usually those of African American descent and people of color) are treated with such rudeness, disdain, hatred, and contempt? Why are we questioned for taking a walk in our own neighborhood? Why, if questioned about being on our own property, not allowed the decency to explain it is our property, until we've been accosted, demeaned, ridiculed, threatened and taken to jail.

Where is the humanity? Where is the love, respect and honor among human beings? Why does the color of a person's skin dictate what type of treatment they receive? I could spout off a lot of statistics right here about the percentage of arrest, bail, pre-trial diversion, plea-bargaining and finally incarceration rates between the various races. I could give case studies about the disparity of sentencing. Fortunately for me that has already been covered by other more talented authors than myself and is not the purview of this work. What I'm simply asking here is where is the humanity?

As I close, I would like to make a couple of recommendations to those who are trying to find solutions to this mess that we are in and when I say we, I mean everyone in this country. If this condition is allowed to continue unchecked and no answers or real solutions are brought forward, this country will implode. People will start to take matters into their own hands. Vigilante squads will start to crop up around this country. Needless people will lose their lives, which will ultimately bring anarchy and usher in martial law.

I would propose peaceful talks between the communities affected by the police shootings and there local government. In cities where the municipal police have abused their authority, conversations with the mayor and city council must take place. Pressure must be put on the city council and mayor to stand with the people to demand that the police chief do either one of two things: either weed out the troublemakers, those that have attacked the concepts of decency and humanity, from their police force or turn in their resignations.

Anyone who has ever been in the military or law enforcement knows that those in command set the tone of the unit. If the commander of the unit does not enforce law and order and require every member to adhere to the rule of the law, you get soldiers or officers interpreting and enforcing laws through their own lens.

District attorneys who are in elected office must hold the police departments accountable to the rule of law. Charges must be brought forth and officers who break the law must be prosecuted fairly. If the D.A. refuses to uphold the oath of his office then the citizens must vote them out and find another candidate who will.

Have the city council, county commissioners and mayor pledge to end corruption in the police and sheriff's departments. If the sheriff's will not clean up the behavior of his deputies, vote him out and elect one that will. If you cannot get support from your local city council that you voted into office and pay their salaries, vote them out.

Finally, if the police chiefs refuse to clean up their departments or turn in their resignations, and the mayor will not remove him from his duties, then the community needs to come together and make a decision. One, either have a recall of the sitting mayor immediately for dereliction of duties and not protecting the safety and welfare of the community or wait until the next election and find another mayoral candidate that will support justice.

We as citizens of the United States have an expectation of fairness and due process from our law enforcement agencies. We also have the law on our side and were reluctantly given a tool to make change, the vote. I believe by exercising our right to vote, backed by a solid strategy, we will **Survive after Being Stopped by the Police.**

In the famous words of the late Rodney King, "can't we all just get along".

E. Niketa Parker is a devoted husband, father and grandfather of 4. He is a Pastor of Living Waters Ministries and is a member of the largest Pentecostal Denominations in the world, The Church of God in Christ. He served as the first black male Probation and Parole Officer in Okaloosa County, Florida. He also served as the first black drug Court Officer for that county which garnered grave reviews for having a successful program and cutting the recidivism rate for repeat offenders. He served as a Missions president and State Evangelist of the Northwest Florida Jurisdiction leading souls to the Lord. He accepted a position with Mead Johnson Nutritional Company and became a top 10% Sales rep in Pharmaceutical Sales. He is a former Executive Board member and President of the Pastors and Elders Council of the Alabama Third Ecclesiastical Jurisdictional. He currently serves as the Superintendent of the Southeast Birmingham District under the Georgia Northern 2nd Jurisdiction.

For more information, questions or appointments, please contact me through;

Website: http://www.enparker.com
Email: eparkertalks@gmail.com
Twitter: @enparkertalks
Facebook: enparkertalks
Speaking engagements upon request